The • Life Cycle • Series

The Life Cycle of a

Snake

John Crossingham & Bobbie Kalman

Crabtree Publishing Company

www.crabtreebooks.com

The Life Cycle Series

A Bobbie Kalman Book

Dedicated by Crystal Sikkens
For my parents, Joyce and Larry,
who have given me endless love and support

Editor-in-Chief
Bobbie Kalman

Writing Team
John Crossingham
Bobbie Kalman

Editorial director
Niki Walker

Editors
Amanda Bishop
Molly Aloian

Art director
Robert Mac Gregor

Design
Katherine Berti
Margaret Amy Salter (cover)

Photo research
Laura Hysert
Crystal Sikkens

Production coordinator
Heather Fitzpatrick

Consultant
Patricia Loesche, Ph.D., Animal Behavior Program
Department of Psychology, University of Washington

Photographs
Erwin and Peggy Bauer: pages 16, 17 (bottom), 18
James Kamstra: pages 10 (bottom), 13 (top), 29 (bottom)Robert McCaw:
pages 24, 25, 30
James H. Robinson: page 31
Allen Blake Sheldon: pages 11, 12 (bottom), 13 (bottom), 17 (top),19, 21
(top), 22, 26 (top), 29 (top)
Tom Stack & Associates: Joe McDonald: pages 7, 12 (top), 27;Mike
Severns: page 21 (bottom)
Visuals Unlimited: Jim Merli: pages 10 (top), 14, 15, 23 (bottom),26
(bottom); John D. Cunningham: page 23 (top)
Other images by Digital Stock, Digital Vision, and Corbis Images

Illustrations
Barbara Bedell: back cover (center), pages 5 (all except Namaqua dwarf
adder and background for rat snake), 6 (Tuatara, chameleon, tortoise,
crocodile), 19
Katherine Berti: series logo, page 4, 5 (Namaqua dwarf adder and
background for rat snake), 9, 11, 16, 25
Anne Gifford: front and back cover title (little snakes), border, page 6
(boa constrictor)
Bonna Rouse: front cover (egg), page 6 (sea turtle)

Crabtree Publishing Company

www.crabtreebooks.com   1-800-387-7650

Printed in the U.S.A./022011/WW20110117

Cataloging-in-Publication Data
Crossingham, John.
  The life cycle of a Snake / John Crossingham & Bobbie Kalman.
      p. cm. -- (The life cycle series)
  Describes how snakes develop from eggs to adults, why they hibernate, the
difference between poisonous and non-poisonous species, how snakes hunt,
and how people can protect them.
  ISBN 0-7787-0660-5 (RLB) -- ISBN 0-7787-0690-8 (pbk.)
1. Snakes--Life cycles--Juvenile literature. [1. Snakes.]
I. Kalman, Bobbie. II. Title III. Series.
  QL666.O6C835 2003
  597.96′156--dc21
                                                          2003001788
                                                               LC

Published in Canada
Crabtree Publishing
616 Welland Ave.
St. Catharines, Ontario
L2M 5V6

Published in the United States
Crabtree Publishing
PMB 59051
350 Fifth Avenue, 59th Floor
New York, New York 10118

Published in the United Kingdom
Crabtree Publishing
Maritime House
Basin Road North, Hove
BN41 1WR

Published in Australia
Crabtree Publishing
386 Mt. Alexander Rd.
Ascot Vale (Melbourne)
VIC 3032

Contents

So many snakes!

Snakes live all over the world—in deserts and rainforests, on plains and mountains, underground, and even underwater! Scientists have discovered about 2,700 different **species**, or types, of snakes. They come in many sizes and colors. Some are as long as 30 feet (9 m), whereas others are only four inches (10 cm) long. Snakes can be brightly or plainly colored. Many snakes have markings or patterns on their bodies. About one-quarter of all snake species are **venomous**, or able to make poison in their bodies. They use venom to hunt and to defend themselves.

western diamondback rattlesnake

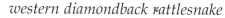

thread snake

garter snake

coral cobra

coral snake

4

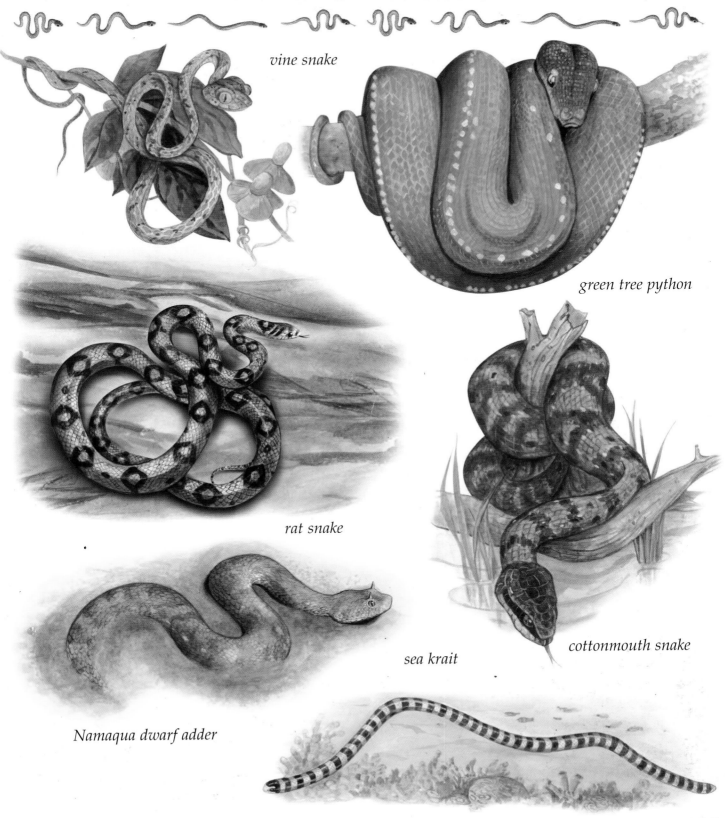

vine snake

green tree python

rat snake

cottonmouth snake

sea krait

Namaqua dwarf adder

What is a snake?

A snake is a legless **reptile**. Reptiles are animals that have backbones and are covered with **scales**, or tuny plates of hard tissue. They breathe air with lungs. Reptiles are **cold-blooded**, which means their body temperatures change as the temperatures of their surroundings change. A snake can raise its body temperature by **basking**, or lying in the sun, and lower it by moving into the shade.

Reptile relatives

There are four main groups of reptiles, as shown here. All these animals share common **ancestors**, or ancient relatives.

boa constrictor

Snakes and lizards belong to the same group. Lizards are the closest relatives to snakes.

chameleon

The tuatara belongs to its own group.

tortoise

sea turtle

Tortoises and turtles have bodies that are encased in hard shells.

crocodile

Crocodiles and alligators are some of the oldest living reptiles. Their ancestors lived during the time of the dinosaurs!

6

*The **Jacobsen's organ** is found on the roof of a snake's mouth. By flicking its tongue, a snake collects scents from the air. It puts them on the Jacobsen's organ to "taste" them.*

*Snakes that live in trees often have **prehensile** tails, or tails that can wrap around and grasp objects. The snakes use their strong tails to grip branches and hang from them.*

*Some types of snakes have small **pit organs** on the sides of their heads. These pits can sense the body heat of other animals, even in the dark.*

A snake's jaws can open wider than the jaws of any other animal.

*Instead of eyelids, each of a snake's eyelids is covered with a single clear scale called a **brille**.*

A snake up close

Many people think snakes are slimy, but their skin is actually dry. Snake skin is made up of two layers: a layer of thin skin covered by tough scales. All the colors and markings are on its scales. The scales help protect the snake's body from drying out. They also help the snake grip the ground when it moves. A snake moves by pushing and pulling its body against the ground or tree bark. When a snake's skin is relaxed, the scales fit together like puzzle pieces. When the skin is stretched, the scales separate. The skin is very strong and can stretch a lot when the snake eats a large meal.

What is a life cycle?

Every animal goes through a series of **stages**, or changes, called a **life cycle**. The cycle begins when an animal is born or hatches from an egg. The animal grows and changes until it becomes an adult. It can then reproduce, or make babies. The babies then start a new cycle. All snakes go through these stages in their life cycles.

What is a life span?

The length of time an animal lives is its **life span**. Most snakes live between ten to thirteen years. They become adults between the ages of one and five years. Large snakes usually have longer life spans than smaller snakes have.

Small snakes usually move through the stages of their life cycles and become adults faster than large snakes do.

The life cycle of a snake

A snake begins its life cycle inside an egg, where it spends several weeks growing. When fully formed, the **hatchling**, or baby snake, breaks out of its egg. It hatches at about the same time as the rest of the eggs in its **clutch** and must then get away from the others quickly to avoid being eaten.

The **juvenile**, or young, snake learns to hunt for food on its own. It grows quickly and **molts**, or sheds, its skin as it gets bigger. Eventually, the juvenile becomes a **mature**, or adult, snake that is able to make babies and start a new life cycle, as shown below.

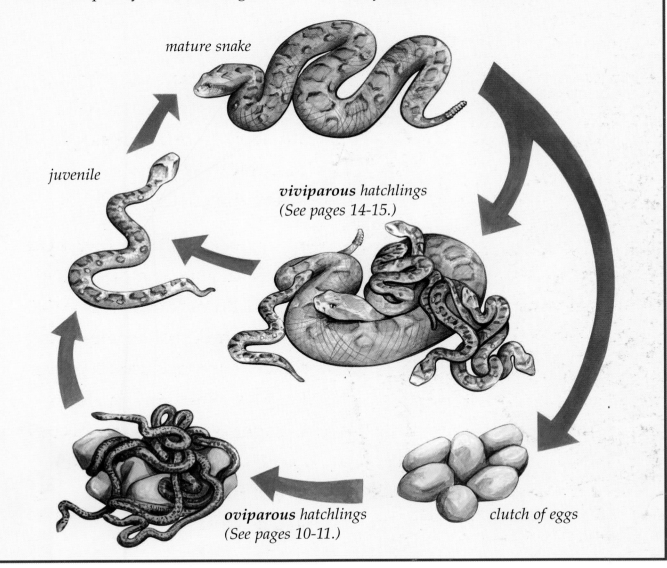

mature snake

juvenile

viviparous hatchlings
(See pages 14-15.)

oviparous hatchlings
(See pages 10-11.)

clutch of eggs

Starting the cycle

*Pythons are the only snakes that **brood**, or rest on their eggs, to keep them warm. Most pythons coil around and over their eggs. They shiver to make heat.*

Most snakes are oviparous, which means they lay eggs. Some females lay only one egg at a time, whereas others lay clutches of more than a hundred eggs! The larger the female is, the more eggs she can produce.

Warm and damp

Before laying their eggs, females must find a good, safe spot. The eggs need to be hidden from **predators**, or animals that feed on them. The eggs also need to be kept warm and moist for the **embryos**, or developing babies, inside to grow. Snakes try to build their nests in damp spots, such as rotting logs and leaf piles. In cool areas, snakes have various ways of keeping their eggs warm. Many cover the eggs with dead leaves and other plant matter to keep out the cold. For more information on where snakes nest, see page 24.

A fox snake has laid its eggs in a dirt pit. It will cover them lightly with dirt to keep them hidden.

Eggs up close

The size of the eggs is different for each species, but most snake eggs are white or cream-colored and oval in shape. Snake eggs do not have hard, brittle shells like those of bird eggs. Instead, they have leathery shells. The shells are **porous**, which means they have tiny holes that allow air and moisture inside.

The size and shape of eggs usually depends on the size and shape of the female laying them. For example, small snakes lay small eggs and thin snakes lay narrow eggs.

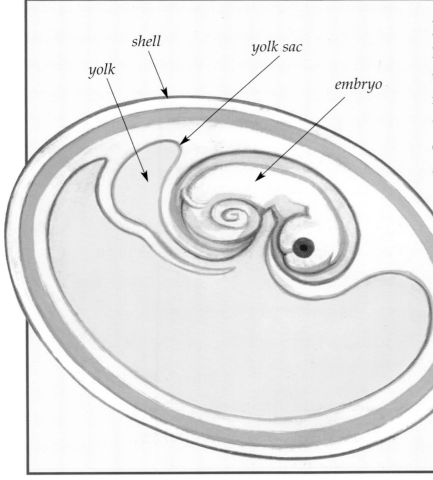

yolk

shell

yolk sac

embryo

Inside the egg

Incubation is the period of time that an embryo spends growing inside its egg. During this time, the egg provides the embryo with everything it needs—food, shelter, and protection. At first, the **yolk sac**, which holds the embryo's food, takes up most of the space inside the egg. As the embryo grows, it feeds on yolk through a slit in its belly and begins to take up more space inside the egg.

By the time it is a few weeks old, a snake embryo begins developing a head, a tail, and eyes.

Out they go

As a snake embryo grows, it needs to breathe more and more oxygen. Eventually, it becomes too large to get enough oxygen through the egg shell. The baby snake must then hatch in order to breathe. Snake eggs usually hatch several weeks after they are laid. All the eggs in a clutch tend to hatch at the same time.

Based on instinct

Breaking through its egg is the first **instinct** a young snake uses in its life. Instinct is a behavior with which an animal is born. A baby snake also has instincts to move and to hunt other animals. As soon as it is born, it is able to defend itself by hissing, striking, or even playing dead! Instinct gives a baby snake a better chance of making it to the next stage in its life cycle.

Baby snakes, such as this timber rattler, can defend themselves and look for food as soon as they hatch.

First moments

A hatchling uses an **egg-tooth** to break through its shell. This tiny, sharp growth on the snake's nose is not an actual tooth. It drops off shortly after the snake hatches. The hatchling does not leave its shell right away. It may spend hours—or even a few days—inside the shell, looking out at its surroundings and living off the rest of its yolk.

This eastern yellow-bellied racer hatchling has used its egg tooth to break through the shell. It may rest for a bit before it leaves the shell.

Born live

Instead of laying eggs, some snakes give birth to live young. These snakes are viviparous. Viviparous snakes include species such as boas, rattlesnakes, and adders. Many aquatic snakes give birth in the water rather than laying their eggs on the ground. Female viviparous snakes carry their eggs inside their bodies, where the eggs are safe from predators. The mothers face new dangers, however. The eggs take up so much room inside their bodies that the mothers cannot eat as much food as they need. They also move slower than normal, making it more difficult to escape enemies.

Unlike oviparous snakes, such as the California king snake and corn snake shown opposite, this eastern garter snake gives birth rather than laying eggs. The newborn garter snake can care for itself immediately.

Carrying eggs

Female viviparous snakes carry from five to 50 eggs inside a body chamber called an **oviduct**. Unlike oviparous snakes, the eggs of viviparous snakes do not have tough shells. Instead, each embryo and its yolk are surrounded by a thin, strong **membrane**, or flexible skin.

Bye bye, babies

The babies in a **litter**, or group, are born at the same time. They are still inside their membranes when then leave their mother's body. The babies use their egg teeth to cut the membranes. The newborn snakes then wriggle free of their membranes and leave their mother immediately.

15

 # Growing up

Baby snakes are on their own as soon as they are born, so they must become good hunters quickly. They begin to catch small **prey** such as insects, snails, frogs, and lizards. They soon grow into juvenile snakes. This stage is a dangerous time for snakes. Many juveniles are eaten by animals such as frogs, eagles, owls, and foxes. When a predator is nearby, the juveniles must be alert and be able to move quickly to avoid being caught. They can escape from enemies by hiding underground or between rocks. For extra protection, some juvenile venomous snakes have venom that is even deadlier than that of their parents. By the end of their first year, juveniles that survive can be up to half their adult size.

A hungry badger will not pass up a chance to attack a juvenile snake.

Different colors

Some juvenile snakes have different colors or patterns than those of adult snakes. For example, a few tree pythons and vipers have green coloring as adults but are bright yellow as juveniles. In general, juvenile snakes are lighter in color than adults are.

Why change?

Scientists have a few ideas about why certain juveniles are different colors than the adults of the same species. Snakes rely on a pigment called **melanin** to produce dark colors in their skins. As snakes grow older, their body produces more melanin, so their color gradually darkens. Younger snakes might also live in different areas than adults do. Their colors and markings help **camouflage** them in their surroundings, just as their parents' camouflage does.

(above) An eyelash viper is bright yellow as a juvenile.

(below) The viper will turn green by the time it is an adult.

17

Outgrowing its skin

A snake's skin does not grow along with its body. As a young snake grows larger, its skin becomes tight. A snake must molt before it can get bigger. A snake first sheds its skin when it is between one and two weeks old.

It then molts three times a year until it becomes an adult. Even as an adult, a snake continues to grow, so it sheds and replaces its skin once or twice a year. The process of shedding lasts four to five days.

A snake that is injured sheds its skin to help repair the damage. Over a period of a few weeks, it may shed several skins to speed up the healing.

Thin skin

A snake actually has two layers of skin—an inner layer that grows along with the snake and an outer layer that is dead. When the snake is ready to molt, it produces a slick liquid between the two layers of skin. This liquid allows the snake to slip easily out of the old skin.

The old dead skin that a molting snake leaves behind is without color or markings.

Get it off!

A snake begins shedding by rubbing the skin around its mouth and head against a rough surface such as a rock or tree bark. Once the skin splits, the snake starts slithering out of it. The old skin usually comes off in one long piece. The snake's new skin is shiny and soft for a few hours after the molt, but it soon dries and hardens. A newer layer of skin begins growing underneath it.

A good home

Almost every snake lives in a **home range**, which is a small territory that it rarely leaves. When a young snake slithers away from its nest, it searches for a home range in which it will hunt and take shelter. Since snakes live in a variety of **habitats**, each snake's home range is a little different.

In the trees

Arboreal snakes live in trees. Many snakes in rainforests are arboreal. By living in trees, they can avoid enemies on the ground. Arboreal snakes use natural **hollows**, or holes, in trees for shelter and nests. The snakes use their prehensile tails to grab and hang from branches.

Many tree snakes are thin and long. Their shape allows them to move easily from branch to branch.

Digging deep

Burrowing snakes live underground. They dig holes called **burrows** in which they sleep and avoid enemies. Burrows also provide shelter from hot or cold weather.

Desert snakes dig burrows in the sand to escape extreme heat.

Up high

A few snakes, such as certain vipers and rattlesnakes, live in the mountains. This environment can be cold, but it is easy for them to find shelter among the rocks and caves on mountainsides.

Many mountain snakes go into deep sleep during the cold winter months.

Under the sea

Aquatic snakes live in water, even though they need to breathe air. Sea snakes can hold their breath for up to two hours! They find shelter along the bottom of oceans or lakes, often between rocks or coral.

Sea snakes live only in tropical areas where the water is warm. They feed mainly on fish and fish eggs.

Making babies

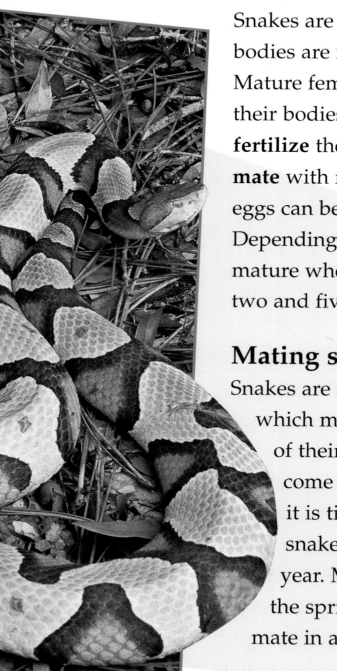

Snakes are mature when their bodies are ready to reproduce. Mature females make eggs in their bodies. Mature males **fertilize** the eggs when they **mate** with females. Only fertilized eggs can become baby snakes. Depending on the species, snakes mature when they are between two and five years old.

Mating season

Snakes are **solitary** animals, which means they spend most of their lives alone. Many come together only when it is time to mate. Mature snakes usually mate once a year. Most snakes mate in the spring, although some mate in autumn.

This mature southern copperhead snake is ready to mate.

Finding a mate

Before they can mate, snakes must find partners. Usually, males go in search of females. When female snakes are ready to mate, they release chemicals called **pheromones**. As the females move, they leave trails of their pheromones, which males follow using their sense of smell. In some snake species, when two or more males find the same female, they may fight for the chance to mate with her.

Some males wrestle when they compete for the same female.

The right time

In spring, females lay their eggs shortly after mating. If snakes mate in autumn, the females store the eggs in their bodies over the winter and lay them in the spring. In areas with very harsh weather or **droughts**, snakes can store eggs for years while they wait for the right conditions to lay them. Viviparous snakes usually give birth a couple months after mating, but they can wait if conditions are not right.

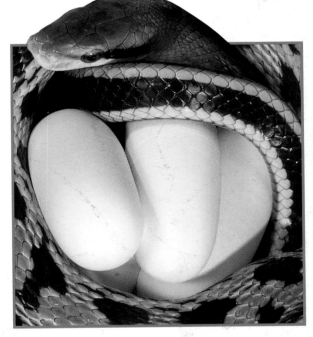

A Taiwan beauty snake coils around the eggs she has just laid.

Safe spots

After mating, oviparous female snakes must begin looking for places to use as nests for their eggs. These spots must be moist, warm, and well-hidden. A female often travels many miles in search of a perfect place. Once she finds a good site, she often returns to the same spot every year to lay her eggs. Excellent nesting sites are used by more than one snake. Sometimes several females share the same nest.

The perfect place

Most snakes lay their eggs in natural holes they find. A few snakes use their snouts to scrape out a pit in soft dirt. Some snakes hide their eggs in caves or under rocks, logs, leaves, or even animal dung! The king cobra is the only type of snake that actually builds a nest by piling up leaves. After laying their eggs, most snakes leave their nests to return to their home ranges.

*This prairie rattlesnake has laid its eggs in a spot similar to the place that it uses for a **den**, or shelter.*

Sleeping through winter

In autumn, snakes that live in places with cold winters must also find safe spots. These snakes enter a deep sleep called **hibernation** to survive the winter. During hibernation, a snake's heart and body functions slow down. It is difficult for a hibernating snake to wake up, so its **hibernaculum**, or hibernating spot, must protect it from predators as well as the harsh weather. Some viviparous species are so well protected in their hibernaculums that they give birth while hibernating. The babies emerge with their parents when the warm weather returns in spring.

Garter snakes often gather in massive groups at the end of autumn. They hibernate underground until spring.

Beating the heat

Like snakes in cold areas, desert snakes enter a deep sleep to escape harsh weather, but they escape extreme heat rather than cold. Their hibernation is called **estivation**. Estivating snakes sleep in burrows deep underground during the hottest part of the year.

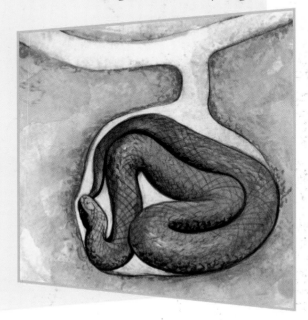

Desert snakes estivate underground for several months a year.

On the hunt

Snakes are predators—they hunt and eat other animals. Depending on their size and where they live, snakes eat mice, lizards, eggs, frogs, birds, pigs, fish, and even other snakes. Snakes always swallow their meals whole and headfirst. They are able to swallow prey that is much larger than themselves.

After constricting a deer mouse, this corn snake begins to swallow its prey.

Many egg-eating snakes have spines inside their throats to crush the eggs before the eggs reach the stomachs of the snakes.

Catching a meal

Some snakes track and **stalk**, or sneak up on, their prey. Some wait in trees and drop onto prey when it passes below them. Others use camouflage to hide and wait for prey to come close. They then **strike** by biting down on the prey quickly. All snakes strike quickly to avoid being hurt by their prey. Snakes use one of two methods to kill prey once they catch it. Some **constrict**, or squeeze, prey. Others poison it with venom.

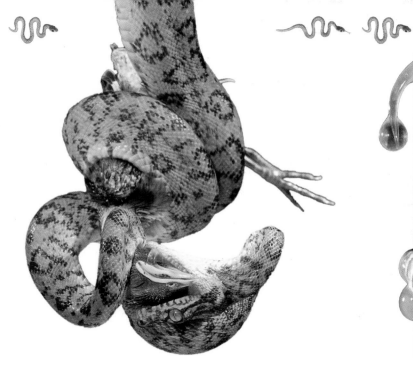

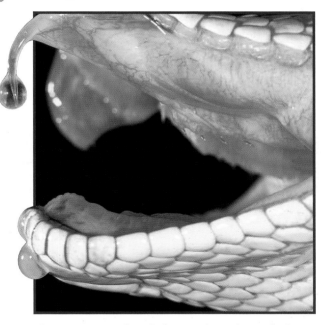

Most snakes constrict their prey. They grab the prey's head in their jaws and wrap themselves around its body. They squeeze tighter and tighter until their prey cannot breathe.

Venomous snakes inject poison into their prey though hollow teeth called **fangs**. Venom usually does not kill prey, but **stuns** prey long enough so a snake can eat it.

Gulp it down!

A snake can take from ten minutes to over an hour to swallow its prey. Once the animal is inside its stomach, the snake slithers away to find a place to rest and **digest**, or break down, its meal. It can take a few weeks to digest a large meal fully, so some snakes need to eat only a few times a year!

While a snake is digesting its meal, it is an easy target for its enemies. It must find a safe place to rest.

Dangers to snakes

The rattlesnake uses its rattle to warn intruders that they are too close. It also uses venom to defend itself.

Snakes are mighty predators, but they can also be prey! Eagles, hawks, large lizards, crocodiles, raccoons, and mongooses are among the many animals that eat snakes. Snakes have developed many defenses to help protect themselves, but they have few defenses against their biggest threat—people.

Snake defenses

A snake's basic defense is hissing. When a snake hisses, it warns other to back off or it will bite. A few snakes, such as cobras, can puff up or spread their necks. These displays make them look larger and more fierce. There are also snakes that pretend to be dead when they are in danger! They roll over, let their tongues hang out, and stay still. Some even release a foul odor that smells like a dead animal.

This cobra spread its hood to look larger. It spits venom toward the eyes of a predator to blind the animal.

The worst enemy

People are the greatest threat to snakes. Each year, they kill thousands of snakes for their skins, which are used to make clothing, boots, belts, luggage, and other items. In some parts of the world, certain snake body parts are used to make medicines, even though there is no proof that these medicines work. People also kill snakes when they clear forests, fields, and other natural areas for construction. Pollution is another threat to the lives of snakes, as it is to the lives of all animals.

Many snakes must be killed to get enough skin to make items such as these boots.

Without the trees in this forest, many of the animals snakes eat are also left homeless. Without homes or prey, entire populations of snakes starve and die.

Helping snakes

Snakes are among the most feared animals in the world, but they are very important to the environment. They are key parts of **food chains** and **food webs**. As predators, they control populations of certain pests, including mice and rats. As prey, they provide food for other animals.

Respect the wild

Snakes may seem frightening, but they are more afraid of us than we are of them! Part of helping snakes is learning to respect them. If you see a snake in the wild, keep your distance and let it be. Snakes have never been known to chase people. Remember, when a snake hisses, it just wants to be left alone.